Release

The Phoenix Trilogy

by

Monica-Grace Mukendi

DORRANCE PUBLISHING CO
EST. 1920
PITTSBURGH, PENNSYLVANIA 15238

Dorrance Publishing Co
585 Alpha Drive
Pittsburgh, PA 15238
Visit our website at *www.dorrancebookstore.com*

ISBN: 979-8-8872-9326-4
eISBN: 979-8-8872-9826-9

Dedicated to ya Sarah for always believing in me
and encouraging me to go after all of my dreams.

"Poem after poem comes — which is perhaps how poets pray"
- Alice Walker

Foreword

I wrote this for you. I wrote this for me. I wrote this for us. To experience the power of release. To put thoughts from my brain to the pen, to the page. To escape. I was running so far from reality that in the process I ran right back in time to where I was supposed to be. I was able to reflect. In the process I turned the hurricane of bottled emotions that seemingly keep me afloat, while also making me feel like I'm drowning, into fresh-water springs (John 7:38 TPT). I wrote this to help point you to a well, from which you can drink and be made well (John 4:10-14 MSG). Key word is, I tired. I hope my hot and cold rain brings you the warmth of a summer breeze on a sunny beach. I hope you find peace (Philippians 4:7 AMP). I hope it takes your breath away and you remember that you can breathe. That you can feel that you can be. That I understand you in a way that maybe no one else could, or no one else did, but I do. I love you (I John 2:2 NIV). I wrote this book to remind you, to remind me, to remind us, that God loves you (Ephesians 3:17 NLT). And by you, I mean me, and by me, I mean us, God loves us (Romans 5:8 AMPC).

The 17/20/23-word poems were born out of a need to speak. During a season when I was unable to utter more than a few words at time.

17-Word Poems

"See Lord, how distressed I am! I am in torment within, and in my heart, I am disturbed." (Lamentations 1:20 NIV)

Speak

Forgive me if I don't speak of myself often;
all I've done in my life is listen

| Lost my voice |

꧁꧂

Despair

The more you wait the more your heart breaks,
but you stay because you're afraid of change

| Despair |

Can you hear

When she found the courage to speak, everyone had gone.
She cried. If only tears made noise.

| Begging to be heard |

The Actress

She can be so many different things
but the hardest thing for her to be, is vulnerable

| Mystique |

Silence

Why must she stay quiet for more than three hours
for you to realize something is wrong

| Oblivion |

20-Word Poems

"Sorrow is better than laughter, for when a face is sad (deep in thought)
the heart may be happy [because it is growing in wisdom]."
(Ecclesiastes 7:3 AMP)

Deception

Your words sting as my mind repeats what I thought was the truth,
I shouldn't have listened

| Reality |

❦

Superpowers

Wishing words had the power to heal broken people like Jean
has the power to heal wounds

| The Phoenix |

Betrayed

I come to you hoping that you help me understand
what's going on in my head; instead you disappoint me.

| i'm talking about poetry, u thought of a person |

❦

Blank

How is it that the mind always seems to run a mile a minute
until it's finally time to speak.

| it's all in our heads |

Family

For weeks you don't get any rain. Then it pours.
Reminding you how water gives life, and can also destroy.

| tears remind me of rain, or vice versa |

Thoughts

I often hear voices that sound like laughter, I often see places
that look like people. I miss both things.

| tearful memories |

Heart

I fight with you every day. You long for a warmth
only a specific pair of hands can provide, I'm sorry.

| like J Cole said 'no heater and I really need heat… may I vent' |

Fraction

I split. Dividing pieces of me for others, holding onto half for myself.
When did I forget how to share?

| when I didn't get myself back |

Introvert

Subconsciously hiding your magical essence, by limiting those
that have the privilege of your existence. Your presence is a blessing.

| allow others to experience it |

🦋

Writing

What do you call, the ability to accurately articulate different human
experiences, and within given parameters. Is it not talent?

| too often we go unappreciated |

23-Word Poems

"For in much wisdom *is* much grief and he who increases knowledge increases sorrow" (Ecclesiastes 1:18 NKJV)

Denial

Sometimes words cut deep. Reaching an unprecedented depth,
it opens up wounds that take lifetimes to heal, I'm not ready to confess.

| it's hard admitting your flaws |

❦

Confused

The mind often wanders even in the presence of love, convincing us
that although we're surrounded, we still need escape.

| the mind and the heart are enemies |

Music

Sometimes, the only time I find solace is in complete solitude,
with tiny speakers in my ears, lyrics speak volumes.

| love note to all lovely notes, thank you |

Dreams

Nighttime, when my eyelids can no longer bare their weight,
they rest, then close. Forgetting that I can still see.

| when do I rest |

Lesson in Grief

Over the years I have found that nothing soothes the heart after loss
like saying I love you. "I'm sorry" only brings tears.

| tell your people you love them |

☙❧

Sleep

Far too often you are used as a means to escape reality
and not as a way for our bodies to physically rest.

| that's why we're always "tired" |

Distance

Avoiding speaking to people you love, seeing people you love, being around
people you love; because around them, it gets harder to pretend.

| can we call this "growth"? |

※※

Reflection

I have always attracted broken people that appear whole.
I think they see themselves in me. I think I see myself in them.

| we can relate |

Irony

Being the one that usually has the right words to say is painful.
If only there was a healthy way to comfort ourselves.

| we can only wish |

❦

Funerals

The loss of a life leaves a gaping hole on the heart,
and sometimes all the empty spaces make it hard to feel whole.

| only the human heart still functions after so much pain |

Instincts

Being surrounded by so much loss so early in life, you become numb.
It is your body's natural response to keep yourself going.

| how do we stop now? |

Maman

Looking in the mirror is a painful reminder of your absence.
Usually just a pinch. But days like this, it's a powerful earthquake.

| it's hard to stand |

Clouds

They are able to acknowledge when they've held too much, they understand the beauty that comes from liberation and the growth that proceeds.

| jealous of their strength |

⚘

Metaphysics

God, if you can't give me heaven, can you at least give me wings?
Even a phone call ... anything to lessen the pain.

| heaven can be a place, heaven can be a person |

The Self Portraits series is a self-reflection prose that allowed me to step outside of myself and look into the mirror. To be objective about myself, my feelings, feelings we all have. Its relatability is only contingent in it being real, it is vulnerability at its peak. This chapter is dedicated to Cristalin who inspired this era and re-cultivated the writer within me.

Self Portraits

"it is like glancing at your face in the mirror. You see yourself, walk away and forget what you look like." (James 1: 23-24 NLT)

Self Portrait in **Heartache**

The Physical Wound

The whole night is dedicated to you. And I wish I meant that in the sweetest way. But I'm in mourning. Grief is heavy. The most powerful emotion, humans are unable to contain it. Nighttime is when I feel it most. When my thoughts aren't running rapid, focusing on a million things. My brain winds down, redirects its focus to one thing. As my body recoils, I become a shell of my emotions. And there you are. I then have no energy to fight away the thoughts and all the pain settles in. Unable to move, I attempt to close my eyes, and you seep into my dreams. A broken bone never truly returns to normal. Likewise, a broken heart. Moving on takes a strength I don't have neither morning, noon, nor night. To pick up the pieces and mend them. A surgery I did not sign up for, I've always hated blood.

The Internal Wound

Realistically, an injury this big needs to be examined multiple times. First it's looked at externally, the physical wound, and then internally. It's still nighttime, and I see you. But this time it's our mini dates. All the places we went, things we saw, things we ate. Then it changes and I can hear every conversation. Your voice alone brings healing to the wound. Just for a second. Before it realizes that none of it is reality. When the facts sink in, we're not in the city on a cold winter night accompanied by the warmth of our laughter, the warmth of your touch. We aren't lying together, a moment of stillness, the most beautiful intimacy, one that doesn't involve sex. We're not looking in each other's eyes feeling as if the world only populates the two of us, the depth of a connection I could never explain. No. Instead, we're surrounded by many. Miles apart and distance only magnifies heartache an injury so grave no doctor has been able to fix.

I feel it the most, but the effects are global. Everyone can feel when a heart is broken. Well, mine, at least, I wear on my sleeve. The worst part about the ache is it comes from someone who I otherwise see as great. The expectations for the next lover continuously climb. I crave that connection. Or something close. People come after, as they always do, and still, nobody is you. From the outside I don't know what it comes off as, maybe cold? But I doubt it. My heart is always warm, even as blood leaks. Still, I know coming in contact with anyone else would mean infecting a fresh wound. Bleeding, on a stranger, inflicting my injury, something I don't want to do. I first need to heal.

Self Portrait in **Affirmations**

Typical Affirmation: *I'm here for you*

Standard for everyone. When anyone is going through anything. I hear it, I say it, and I embrace it, knowing its half the truth even when I say it. I like to hear it, I like to say it, I am here, but am I really? I can't be here and you can't be here. When I am here, I am open I am receptive and everything you feel sets in, settles deep into my pores. I spew emotion. Yours and mine. So me being here, fully here, I lose my mind. Which is also typical. So, I mean, I embrace it. I tell the truth when I say I am here. You? I can't be sure. But I say it so you know, I am here.

Typical Affirmation: *It'll get better, I promise*

The last time I meant this was probably years ago. Life has been unkind. Sometimes I hear things where no response is adequate. There is nothing to say, and before I knew the power of silence and presence in place of an empty promise, I gave what I thought was hope. Until it didn't get better. Until it always got worse. Talking to myself. Talking to others.

Common Affirmation: *I'm sorry*

For this no explanation is due, we should all understand. But when put in place of the promise of a better outcome it is counterproductive. I don't know what is going to happen. I don't know what to do to make you feel better, and it hurts me that I cannot do more, that I can't ease your pain. But I don't know if I am affirming you or excusing my lack of ability to affirm you. I will try to be better. I'm —-

Self Portrait in **Prayers**

Prayers in Psalms

Before I realized how powerful this book in the Bible was, all I did was recite this verse. Psalms 23. I thought "my birthday is on the 23rd, God wants me to know this!". I closed my eyes and repeated the words with no regard for the actual meaning of the words. I regurgitated the words the lines the verses and knew nothing but the fact that it relaxed me. I was content with this.

Prayers and Loss

I will never forget the days I prayed for someone to survive. I wrote the prayers down and even wrote a poem. My anxiety was through the roof, but I was told that God is greater, to rest and pray. I didn't rest, but I prayed, and at the funeral I remembered that prayer. I remember looking up into the sky and feeling like God failed me. When my aunt passed away, a God-fearing woman of compassion and wit, I remembered that prayer. This time, I couldn't look up to the sky, I could only cry. Yet somehow, at some point, I felt a shift. A sense of comfort. My anxiety was relieved when I realized that everyone I had loved that went to heaven helped to anchor me on earth. Ironically, loss brings me light because it leads me to Christ. I only find solace in knowing that they have God in them. That same God lives in me, and that same God lives in you.

Prayers in Trains

I spent lots of time on the train. Oftentimes, my mind wandered. On one of those days, tears filled my eyes. That was the first time I prayed. "God, I can't stop crying," I said "I write this as tears filled my eyes." I prayed every single day. My voice speaks through writing. I wrote every single day.

Prayers as a Coping Mechanism

I have had anxiety for as long as I can remember. Before every test my heart would run skip and jump. I recited, regurgitated, repeated "God grant me the Serenity to accept the things I cannot change, the Courage to change the things I can, and the Wisdom to know the difference". Then I could begin. On days I knew there was trouble, "Although I walk through the valley of the shadows of death I fear no evil for You are with me". And I feared less, and my anxiety left for a split second. But it never fully leaves does it.

Prayers as a Voice
My aunt, God rest her soul, told me prayer is supposed to be a conversation between you and God. The same way you talk to your friends about everything, you should be able to talk to God about everything. I never told anyone everything, but I suppose God already knew. I was embarrassed. I came to God apologizing, I'm sorry for, I'm sorry for. But God isn't like everyone else, I didn't have to walk on eggshells and apologize. God loved me. God loves me. There nothing I could do to change that. I felt free and that allowed me to find my voice and finally speak.

Praying in Church
The first time I came back to church I felt out of place. An individual, in a room full of strangers, yet they saw me as family. I was uncomfortable; all the hugging and the touching, the affection was a lot to take in. I sat down. Praise and worship was fine I stood and clapped. I listened to the message for tithe and offering, I listened to message for the service. Everything was fine until it was time to pray. I never prayed in front of people. I looked around, and no one was paying attention to me. I closed my eyes and spoke. Perhaps in that moment I was transformed.

This chapter is a compilation of old poems that still showcase a significant part of myself. It shows how my relationship with poetry has changed, how much I engaged with the craft in a way that was elementary as opposed to sincere and true. How afraid I was and sometimes still am of vulnerability, of freedom, honesty, and truth. It shows how much I perform daily to uphold this persona that I built around my presence. Yet I can't be present in the given circumstances, that's an actor's reference, but I hope you get it. This chapter shows how I was depressed. It shows the pressure that built up before the Phoenix erupted. I was in love, I was lost, I was confused, I was sad. I was in transition. The process of understanding myself in order to explode and become transformed, grow, learn. But most of all, for most of the time, I existed outside of myself and the only place I made an attempt at being me was through this poetry. I was hesitant to release them because I read them and felt cringe, embarrassment, and shame. But if it can brighten someone's day to have them know they aren't alone, at least it has done its job. I call this chapter "Shedding," because I am no longer holding on to them. This is me, letting go. The Phoenix has to shed to begin the process of transformation. So, I have to let go, to release, to truly to be free, and be reborn into who I was always destined to be. Whose I was always destined to be.

Shedding

"Who has woe? who has sorrow? who has contentions? Who has complaints, who has wounds without cause? who has redness of eyes?" (Proverbs 23:29 NKJV)

Okay-? Okay.—.

Let's sit together
And stare at the stars
Talk about
Who we are
Not as a couple
But individually
I want you
To be able to know me, —
So well that I don't have to say a word
And you know everything that's going on in my head
I wanna know you
The deeper, darkest sides
I want to cherish this bond
Be glad our paths were able to collide
But let's not only speak of the bad
Our silence is understood by each other
There's a mutual understanding
A connection between lovers
Let's lie in bed, —
Let's be together
So that even for a second
We can forget —
Forget the world
We can focus on
This perfect moment we have
Together

Oxymoron

She could walk 1,000 miles
On shattered pieces
And fix every person
That was shattered to pieces
She could hand them an umbrella
To walk through the rain
She could change their whole life
But that wouldn't ease the pain
And although she helped them change
She'd still feel the same

Numb

From the outside
She seems focused in her head
She pays attention to you
Remembers what you said
Laughs with you
Giggles and smiles
She can hold conversation
A heart to heart
For more than a lil' while
But as the conversation goes on
If you pay really close attention
You can see theres something wrong
And she's not so strong
But she'll never cry
You won't see a single tear shed
Because in her mind
Her emotions have disappeared

Sleep

You know that feeling
When you just can't be strong
When everything's all right
But at the same time everything's all wrong
Where you feel so empty
So dark
You can't describe
What's running through your mind
Where you just want to sit and cry
Where the tears aren't coming out
Where you can't open your mouth
Where your heart wants to speak
But you don't know what to say
So instead
You
Just
Sleep

Light

You are
My favorite hello
Whether your day is high
Or it's kind of low
You got that kind of presence
That makes people cherish
Every word down to the syllables
You put a smile on my face
That all day I can't shake
You ride for me
You cry for me
Hand on the Bible
You'll lie for me
Ask for forgiveness later
You're a crazy one
No one can really tame you
But I don't even want to
Who would you be
If we took the spark in your eye
The passion that shines
Like stars in the sky
You're a star yourself
And in this world
There are only a few good ones left
Stars bring out the best in you
Stars really test you
Stars help you be yourself
Kind of allow you to soften
But they shine the best
In darkness

So there may be times
When stars clash
When stars crash
Some stars may fall
Some stars will last
But at the end of the day
Everything is better in twos
And this star
Shines brighter
With
You

Broken

And it's sad to say
That no matter what is said
Her tears kept falling
And her soul always bled

Detached

In a room filled with people
She felt disconnected
In crowd filled with laughter
All she felt was rejected
Like her body and mind
We're not intertwined
It was a feeling
She couldn't define
Like although she was laughing
She genuinely smiled sometimes
In her heart she knew she wasn't fine
It was like the hollowest hole
And she wanted so badly to be filled and made whole
She emptied herself
For the happiness of others
Waiting for the day
At least one person would do the same
It's how she spent her days
And she had nobody to blame
But herself
And maybe there's comfort in loving yourself
But she couldn't do it
Yes, she tried
But every time she attempted to look in the mirror
All she could do was cry
If only mirrors didn't show imperfections
But were actually
your soul reflected
And even then all she would see is dark
Because although she had a heart of gold
All she ever felt in her soul
Was cold

Lost

And the scariest thing is
Whether we know it or not
We were all
In a way
Drifting

The Giver

I am the girl who waters the plant too much because I can never stop giving
I am that girl who cries
When it dies
And thinks it's my fault
I was never taught to receive
All I know is to please
Pour yourself in everything you love
That's what was said to me
So I can't believe that you'd question
How I became so empty
My soul is trapped yet it keeps on leaving
I'm awake in a world where I just want to keep dreaming
The pain of being caged but the fear of freedom
Is just too much to take
If you escape, the world captures your soul
Caring about yourself is selfish and painful too
You could never treat others
The way they treat you continuously taking never pouring in
You only know how to make others happy
I guess that's the "gift"
Of being born a giver

Shadow work

Misery likes company
So I allowed it to stay
But it couldn't just sit around
It crawled up next to me
It reminded me
Of so many terrible memories
I try to run away and scream, tears running down my cheeks
It stopped and it touched me
I burst into tears
Worried that it knew all of my fears
It touched my skin
It crawled up my arms, reached my face, and tried to get me to swallow some-
thing
It tasted like the truth
I swallow my fate
Obeying its orders
Even though this feels like a dream
I close my eyes to sleep
My favorite way of escaping reality
My whole body shakes, this thing is keeping me awake
I stopped fighting after awhile
And It just left
Idk why it came
But I knew after that encounter
I would never be the same
The pain of its presence was actually a present
because it reminded me, I was human
I could cry, I could feel
It is what ultimately helped push me to heal

Lost

She's In Over Her Head
No one Understands
She's Sinking
And Has No Plan
She Can't Be Saved
She Sits And Prays
As She Begins To Shed A Tear
All She Feels is Like Her Soul Is Slowing Going To Disappear

Silence

I've honestly been silenced for as long as I can remember
Sometimes I would cry
Because I wanted to say something so badly
I don't remember ever using my voice
I could talk for hours about meaningless things
And nothing was said
But when I really wanted to speak
When I really needed to be heard
When I wanted to say I was hurt
When I wanted to say I was sad
I was told never complain about things I couldn't change
But I just wanted to explain
How sometimes I lay in bed at three a.m. wide awake
Sometimes my whole body grows cold
Sometimes I get goosebumps
Sometimes I want to cry and I can't
Sometimes I feel things
And I don't know why
Sometimes my friends
Remind me of how broken I am
Because I know they can't understand me
They don't understand themselves
I understand them
I don't understand myself
Sometimes I get this cloud over me
And my heart feels like it folds
Sometimes I want to scream what's wrong with me
Sometimes I think it should be just as easy to talk about myself as it is for others
Sometimes I think if you know too much you'll leave
Sometimes I think you wouldn't love me

Sometimes I find that voice
That was lost while screaming
That was lost while trying to keep from crying
That was lost while hoping
That was lost with my innocence
I thought speaking would be the death of me that no one would believe me
That to be loved was to never mention too much about yourself
Emotions are too much,
vulnerability is too much,
the weight of your sadness is too much, it scares people away
So, to keep people close I never say too much and
although I engage in conversation
my heart sits in silence
Waiting for the courage to finally speak

This chapter is an extension of the first. This type of shedding is like peeling an onion. It hurts. There are layers, and there are tears. But we embrace the versatility of the onion, its ability to elevate any dish is astonishing. It adds that little dash, that pinch, to put it all together into something so amazing you forget that in its raw state it made you cry. I hope I can do the same for you in this chapter.

Shedding II

"Lord, listen to my cry; give me the discerning mind you promised"
(Psalm 119:169 NLT)

Healing

My heart is heavy

With no explanation

With so many parts in so many places

It's hard to keep track

The body is familiar with trauma

So when its triggered it protects itself

And it goes back to what it is used to

What normally brings healing

But those methods are defective and going back to them makes you disappointed

You feel like the growth you thought you made was a delusion

Depression feels like regression

Even if only for a day

It feels like you've lost the race

But God promised rebirth

And women have seldom given birth

Without shedding tears

And yet still suffering is forgotten

When the miracles arrives

And even though the body remembers the trauma

It heals

Reminding you of your strength

So forgive yourself for moments of supposed weakness

Embrace it as vulnerability

Know that when you are dealing with open wounds

Growth will feel like pain

But pain is proof that healing is taking place

Longing

To be in love
And young
To be embraced
To be held
To be appreciated
To see wonder in
To be beauty in
To never want to be away from
To always want to know more about
Dig deeper into
Explore more
Find more
Enjoy more
Dream more
Plan together
Love together
Make together
Break together
Cry together
Talk together
Forgive together
Grow together
Stay forever
Companionship forever
I want

Cycle

Is failure inevitable?
I mean for everyone who has tried and yet still has succumb
To the weight of their childhood
Kids, they have hope
When they're broken
They have time to heal and be whole
Adults, it seems, it's too late
As if the repetition of our guardians is truly just our fate
Fulfilled
How do we overcome?
How do we stop ourselves from becoming numb
How can we turn back time
Rescue those broken children
Who comfort broken adults
I wonder
In whose arms do they cry
Late at night
Partnerless
Fatherless
Motherless
Where do they find joy
To whom shall they seek
When their outwardly strength makes it impossible to seem weak
To break apart
To show their heart
And all its wounds
Who mends all that they resent
Who can touch scars from which they have never spoken
Secrets that will never be unfolded
Who helps them mourn

Who is their healer
When their guardian angels are internally broken themselves
And when open wounds collide the scars only continue to divide
Split
All the way open
Bleeding until there's nothing left
And everyone's empty
Let us learn to be open with our wounds
So we can heal instead of bleed
Together

Suppress

Holding things in is my specialty
I do it so well it feels second nature
People see it as my superpower
And forget to consult me before taking pieces of me
Unknowingly
Breaking me apart
Not knowing the inside
Is soft to the touch
Easy to tare
Easy to tears
I didn't shed today
But I should've
To water the broken soil that is within my soul
And allow for the rebirth I been praying about

Cleanse

Chaos and clutter
Makes my mind wander
I wonder
How do people get out of bed
What motivates them to move?
I get a wind of productivity
Then it fades
As the day withers away
What have I gotten done?
I wonder
How you keep your thoughts from creating a mess in your room
In your house
How does one keep the mind clean
I've been cleansing
using the Lysol, searching for bleach
I want to be present
But I'm elsewhere right now
And I can't figure out how
To keep it together and stay in one piece
I guess I'm still searching
For peace

Still

Still need a grasp on handling emotions
Still need help staying focused
Still need a break every now and then
Still need someone to hold my hand
Still need everyone to let me go
Still need someone to hold me close
Still need space to make mistakes
Still need air
Still need grace
Still need familiar faces that feel like home
Still need home
Still need to be alone
Still need comfort
Still need love
Still need God
Still need

Captivated

I know I'm a dreamer
I daydream and dream at night
During both times it's love at first sight
I see you and I'm mesmerized
Forgotten about all toxicity
I stare into your eyes
I feel the love
The butterflies in my stomach take flight
It's as if all the pain was worth it
All the wait was worth it
All the weight was worth it
It is fate
It's you and me
Even for just this moment
Let me enjoy it

Wait for It

It's easier to reflect
With a paper and a pen
Easier to deflect
Easier to forget
Easier to imagine
Easier to dream
Wait for it
Close your eyes
Allow the mind to wander
It often takes you to a place where you physically can't go
Reality drifts away
And we're here
Creating the life we want
Expressing yourself is easy when you are alone
With your thoughts
Left to your devices so you can just dream
Let's escape
Together
Let's create
Together
Let's live
Together
I can't do it without you
I'm willing to wait for it
I wait for it
But it never comes
How quickly joy escapes
When the poem is done
You're just left numb
Happiness is fleeting
Constantly left
Waiting for it

Paint the Pain

I woke up at three a.m. and realized
That without poetry I wouldn't know my feelings
I suppress so much I convince myself nothing is there
But lately I've been feeling
And the feelings are too overwhelming to feel
Like my whole body could explode
It's things that I know
And the things I don't
Things too afraid to admit
Or too afraid to submit to God
like acknowledging is synonymous to drowning
I used to know how to swim
But lately when I'm in the water my body is unable to move
it forgets how to
and it's easier to drown
I forgot how to swim
but my thoughts learned to fly
I wish I could cry
I wish I could escape
I know there is comfort in releasing
I know it is enough to make me whole
but I can't afford to be broken
Can't afford to crack
The vulnerability, the tears, the weight of it all makes me sink
Into a hole that takes forever to crawl out of
The fight is exhausting
It's easier to write
But even writing gets fuzzy
when the topic isn't pretty, poetry is depressing,
so we dress it in metaphors, layer some similes, drop in some imagery

Paint the pain
illustrate the truth in a picture palatable for you
Not for us
The poets
I woke up at three a.m. and realized
Without poetry
I feel nothing

The onion is still peeling. I hope you can trust the process and see that there is a progression and growth. This is the chapter of an unexpected growth. It shows how God is so infinite in his wisdom that everything perfectly falls into place. The seventeen-word poem about clouds turned into a prose from which the title of this book was birthed. Likewise, the name of this sequential love story, "The Phoenix Trilogy," was birthed from a story I long loved but reaffirmed by a poem written in this time. Every Sunday, after I prayed, I would write. Kendra and I would exchange poems, who knew my afternoon thoughts would be words on these pages. Thank you God. Thank you Kendra.

Shedding III: Sunday Poems

"Out of the depths, I cry to you, Lord; Lord hear my voice"
(Psalms 130:2 NIV)

Enough

I don't write enough
I don't share enough
I talk too much
I don't talk enough
I think too much
I don't think enough
I miss you too much
You don't miss me enough
I think about you too much
I don't think about myself enough
I daydream too much
I lay awake too much
I sleep too much
I don't sleep enough
I believe in love,
a little bit too much
I believe in love
But sometimes
love isn't enough
I attach things to you
I have attachment issues
Too many issues
I write too much
I don't write enough

Untitled

I am naturally indecisive
Or so I think
I feel like I wasn't born with the ability to be quick to choose
It takes so much for me to make a choice
I think about everything
Weigh everything
Envision everything
Predict the outcome for everything
Predict reactions for everything
Predict the ending of everything
I don't like surprises
I like to know everything
Except
With love
I don't think about everything
I enjoy everything
The little things
The big things
I like the newness of everything
Getting to know everything
Asking questions about everything
Finding similarities in everything
Finding the joys in everything
Being able to laugh about everything
Seeing the person in everything
Finding connections in everything
Seeing the light in everything
Light is everything
Connections are everything
Love is everything

Fire

When you love like fire
You often get misused
Damaged, discouraged, tossed away
Abused
When you love like fire
You draw people close
Attracted to your warmth
Your light
They've been in darkness too long
You feel like hope
When you love like fire
You help cultivate
Create
Empower
Beautify
Fire gave birth to a revolution
A shift in generation
The cornerstone of civilization
Your love is revolutionary
But when you love like fire
You burn
people
easily
You rush towards companionship
Your love is engulfing
People burn easy
And you end up alone
So don't love like fire

The Attic

Ghosts of the past live here,
Inside my mind.
Stored in the part of the brain that holds memories and pain
Ghost of the past live here, we live together.
We are housemates we are co-laborers,
Yet they feel welcomed while I feel like I am trapped.
An endless cycle of sweeping up their mess,
my mess,
our mess,
a mess!
The ghost fills up the space so we can't have visitors,
there is no joy.
They recount conversations and replay moments
while tears steam down my eyes.
It's an overwhelming sadness.
No matter how many times I try to clean, the ghosts never leave.

An Ode to Poetry

I honestly and truly hate you
The fact that you can give me so much to say
While also leaving me speechless
It baffles me
Why?
The fact that you can make me feel everything all at once
And nothing at all
Numb
I been searching for my voice
I really miss you
You help me understand myself
Life is null and void, it lacks expression
I'm less expressive
But also more explosive
You help control me
In a healthy way
You give me hope
I cope
With loss
With anger
Disappointment
From people I love
From strangers
Frustration
From everything
You frustrate me
I just want you
To want me
I want
to be able

to write
Poetry
Ironically, I just did
I guess this is your way of coming back to me
I promise to be a better host
To nourish and cultivate you
Water you so we can blossom
Welcome home

Looking for joy

I wake up in the morning and immediately feel your absence,
replaced with fatigue and unrecalled dreams,
I miss you.
The way you caused my body to rise without alarm
like the sun, every morning you kissed me
reminding me that amidst my fatigue I could tackle the day
that whether I slept or not I would rise.
You taught me to smile you encouraged me
you said to me
the most important thing I could do for others was to take care of myself
You taught me comfort in being alone
I didn't crave anyone other than you.
But I took you for granted
Didn't hold you in my grip when I noticed you slipping
I let you walk
You were almost out the door when I began chasing after you
But you seemed to have made up your mind
The faster I ran to catch you the quicker you pulled away
I miss you
Days are heavy
nights are heavy
my body is heavy
without you,
I'm empty
I still look for you in the sun
but when I look up it blinds me
I think that's your way of telling me you left me
you've left me behind
and yet still
I look

Phoenix

Does the Phoenix exist?
The bird that burned
Consumed by fire
And went through rebirth
Is it true?
That she exuded the sun's rays
Engulfed by its rage
And was still reborn
Made a new
Is it true?
Well, I believe she does
Because when I look in the mirror
I see her in you

Release

I wrote a poem about clouds

How jealous I am of their strength

I said,

"They are able to acknowledge when they've held in too much

They understand the beauty that comes from liberation and the growth that pro-

ceeds"

I described

In twenty-three words exactly the type of person I would've been

Had I not had an early encounter with death

They call it trauma, a death,

A physical injury

What would come of the earth if God decided to take a cloud away from its

cluster

Have you noticed clouds move in a pack

Gracefully

They synchronize

Like the removal of one could mess up their musical piece

Peace

Who would lead once one is gone

How do they continue to move about following the sun in perfect rotation

But they would

Clouds were equipped to handle the most catastrophic of natural disasters

Unlike us

Unlike me

We become traumatized

A physical injury

Keeping a tight grip on everything because that's what keeps it from running

That's what keeps it from leaving,

That's what keeps the blood from leaking,

I tremble at the thought of losing grip and bleeding out

The trauma warps my sense of reality
I forget some wounds can't heal without breath
Can't heal without air
Can't heal with my grip
Including me
Especially me
I have to take a lesson from these clouds
Of the healing that comes from release

Afterword

"I know I distressed you greatly with my letter. Although I felt awful at the time, I don't feel at all bad now that I see how it turned out. The letter upset you, but only for awhile. Now I am glad — not that you were upset, but that you were jarred into turning things around. You let the distress bring you to God, not drive you from him. The result was all gain, no loss. Distress that drives us to God does that. It turns us around. It gets back in the way of salvation. We never regret that kind of pain. But those who let distress drive them away from God are full of regrets, end up on a deathbed of regrets. And now, isn't it wonderful all the ways in which this distress has goaded you closer to God? You're more alive, more concerned, more sensitive, more reverent, more human, more passionate, more responsible. Looked at from any angle, you've come out of this with purity of heart. And that is what I was hoping for in the first place when I wrote the letter. My primary concern was not for the one who did the wrong or even the one wronged, but for you—that you would realize and act upon the deep, deep ties between us before God. That's what happened—and we felt just great." (2 Corinthians 7:8-10 MSG)

Author's Note

Dear reader,

First of all, I love you (Ephesians 3:18-19 NLT). Not just you today, or future you, but younger you. That's who I am speaking to today. That inner child that was neglected in whichever way affects you. I want you to know that you are light to this world. Your existence is evidence of the love of God personified. I love you (1 Corinthians 13:4-9 NIV). I know that you are hurting from so many things, too many things to sit here and name but I love you (1 John 4:21 TPT) so much and I wish my love could cover the pain (I Peter 4:8 AMPC). Mine can't but I know God can (Romans 8:39 AMP). I know that others don't see the imprint of the pain they caused, and yet you have to live with that. I know that it's hard for you to admit that you've been hurt, it's easier for you to put others first and invalidate yourself. Your pain is valid, no matter how minuscule it may seem to others if it hurts you, it hurts me, and I am sorry. I am sorry that you feel like you have to hide so many things, I am sorry that you felt the weight of adult problems at such a young age. I am sorry you spent so long trying to understand and get over it instead of just being a kid. I'm sorry your childhood was robbed from you by the realities of this world. I'm sorry your emotions never got to grow even though you did. I'm sorry you had to pretend to have it all together for so long. You can fall apart now. It's okay to make mistakes we all have (Romans 3:23 NKJV). You're not perfect but you deserve to be loved not because of what you do or don't do because of who you are. Because of whose you are (Galatians 4:7 NLT). Despite whoever rejects you, you are chosen, you are loved (I Peter 2:4 NIV). But I know it hurts, so allow yourself to go through the emotions and let it all out. I give you permission to grieve, to cry, to scream to be unraveled (Psalms 9:9-10 MSG). True strength is in weakness (2 Corinthians 12:9 NLT). I'm sorry you felt rejected, unworthy, unloved, and never enough. I'm here to tell you, you are more than enough. You are fearfully and wonderfully made (Psalm 139:14 NKJV). I'm sorry you felt so ashamed. I'm sorry you felt you had to hide the parts of yourself that you thought no one would accept. You are a city on a hill that cannot be hidden (Matthew 5:14 NLT). You are amazing. Every part of you. Even the parts you were afraid to show, where all you see is darkness, I see beauty. I'm sorry you didn't feel seen, like truly seen. I see you all of you and I love you (1 John 4:18 NIV). And although your pain may feel never ending right now you will make it to the other side. You have survived all of your bad days and you will continue to do so. I believe in you. I know you will go on to do amazing things (Proverbs 31:29 NIV). I love you (1 Corinthians 16:14 NKJV). I know you will go on to heal others by revealing your story. I know you were born to change the world. Although it may not look like it, all things work together for the good (Romans 8:28 NLT), because God loves us (John 3:16 NIV). So, amidst all the chaos I see you as a masterpiece. I love you (1 Corinthians 13:13 NLT). This is only the start but at least you are on a path to heal. We are on the path of healing. All your pain has purpose. Your breath is evidence of your purpose. I'm proud of you for daring to be vulnerable and committing to releasing your emotions and embracing your humanity. I encourage you to continue to feel, to cry, to laugh, to have fun! Enjoy the highs the lows the mundane, live in the moment. Experience life don't get stuck looking at life through a lens of trauma (Ecclesiastes 3:1-8 NIV). There's beauty to behold in the present so be bold enough to seek it. I promise to continue to pour into you and nurture your soul. I encourage you to reread this letter a few times, anytime you feel you need it. Read it out loud to yourself and believe it. In reading, I hope you see the beauty we create when we embrace all parts of ourselves and drink from the well of the Living Water to begin the journey of being made whole. I wrote this to me. I wrote this to you. I wrote this to us.

Closing Prayer

"I pray that He would unveil within you the unlimited riches of His glory and favor until supernatural strength floods your innermost being with His divine might and explosive power. Then by constantly using your faith, the life of Christ will become the very source and root of your life. Then you will be empowered to discover what every holy one experiences—the great magnitude of the astonishing love of Christ and all it's dimensions. How deeply intimate and far-reaching is His love. How enduring and inclusive it is! Endless love beyond measurement that transcends our understanding—this extravagant love pours into you until you are filled to overflowing with the fullness of God! Never doubt God's mighty power to work in you and accomplish all this. He will achieve infinitely more than your greatest request, your most unbelievable dream, and exceed your wildest imagination! He will outdo them all, for His miraculous power constantly energizes you. Now we offer up to God all the glorious praise that rises from every church in every generation through Jesus Christ—and all that will yet be manifest through time and eternity. Amen!" (Ephesians 3:14-21 TPT)